Once upon a time on Christmas day, this old lady was abandoned by her children that she loved. They refused to help her. They left her alone in a rocking chair with her dog and walked away.

She got out. No money for rent, draging her rocker and a blanket.

She cam upon an old farm and seen a broken down shed to sleep in with her dog in the hay. They kept each other warm.

Now across the street is a different story. The bells are ringing and the stockings are hung and carolers are at the door singing. Everyone is having a good time.

Whoops, Santa slipped down the chimney head first. Meanwhile the Reindeer were laughing until he came back up.

Grandma's cookies are done. Grandpa is sharping his knife to carve the turkey. The smell of good food is filling the air.

The aroma smell got in the old lady's shed from across the street while she was eating her cold beans in a can.

Meanwhile the dog was digging for a bone in the yard.

The poor old lady had raw hands and knees from scrubbing floors for a living. I know children in orphanages that would be more then happy to help her, if she was there own.

One night looking up at the clouds she saw a castle in the sky. She fell to her knees and cried.

Please God look my way and don't forget me like my children did.

Then it happen,
Out of nowhere, Bill appeared. He even had a wooden leg and a banjo.

He bought the farm and built himself a one room shack with a stove to keep warm.

Bill found the old lady sleeping in the hay with her dog.

He invited her in as a good friend to stay.

They help each other out filling potato sacks with hay for beds.

Bill was all heart. He help to build a Church in his small town.

On the weekends Bill would sing and play his banjo in the streets. The dog would keep watch over the donations in the can.

The donations were used to bake bread.

Flo, the old lady that Bill found in the shed, is really a good cook.

Bill would go around town and give the bread away to the people on the streets.

Bill also went fishing and he was blessed

with an awful lot of fish of which he

shared as well.

So Bill took the fish to the church. He found a lot of people there. He shared his fish with them too.

Bill went out side and even tended to the

ministers horse that had a cut from a fence.

The minister was new to the small town. They started chatting about there past and found out that Bill was actually his lost brother.

Bill shared that he is a veteran and that he served in the last war.

This how Bill lost his leg in a helicopter crash.

So Christmas dinner is bread and fish. A store bought chicken, a big bone for the dog and marshmallows strung all over the old tree.

The wish bone was hung on the wall for answers of prayers from God.

Bill on his Banjo with lady in her rocking chair.

Happy together singing Christmas songs.

Bill asked Flo to marry him. His new found brother, the minister held the ceremony in the new church. His brother blessed their marriage to one another.

It may not of been the castle she saw in the sky. But Heaven on Earth it was her dream come through.

Merry Christmas

and

God bless.

Story was written and illustrated by:

Flossie Langdon Ward

About the author:

Flossie is 87 years old and was born in Ontario, Canada in October of 1927.

Published in agreement with:

Createspace Inc.

www.ingramcontent.com/pod-product-compliance
Lightning Source LLC
Chambersburg PA
CBHW041552220426

43666CB00002B/49